Be literate to re iterate experiences

SundayInk

EXPERIENTIAL TOUR

Shrenik S Shah

CONTENTS

BUSINESS STRENGTH

FOREWORD

(Dr. D Bhalla, IAS Retd.)

As I write this foreword, I am remembering my own experience as a student of management and then as a practitioner of various concepts of management, theory and principles in my work in the field of governance and administration. This book by **Shrenik Shah** has resonated with me deeply and is a meticulous compilation of his innovative tools and techniques developed by him during his pioneering journey in the field of financial crime prevention and help organizations and enterprises minimize unnecessary losses.

Negotiation mastery is the mastering of skills to maximize the value in the agreement we reach-soft skills, inter personal skills, interactive skills, emotional intelligence as a crucial skill in negotiation process, the whole world of negotiations is opened up by the author besides a great exposition of the whistle blowing concept and process. Data is the new gold is an often repeated phrase now but the author's exposition of data, its potential for innovation, generating of insights by data, data being essential for training AI models unblocking of full potential of data, management of data, the data ecosystems, challenges to data use, the concept of process and potential of data mining, all this being expounded in a lucid style and in simple text is the specialty and uniqueness of this book.

Art of budget creation is another dimension well explored by the author. I have known the author for a decade and I am privileged to write foreword to his current book which I think will help and assist students, academicians and practitioners equally well!

(Dr. D. Bhalla IAS Retd. is presently serving as an advisor to the Govt. of Nagaland and is a luminary administrator from 1986 batch of IAS, having served 33 years in the distinguished service of nation, postgraduate of public administration, business administration and doctorate in tourism, an author of eight books on topical issues).

It is with immense pride and profound emotion that I write this foreword for a book that holds a special place in my heart. Shrenik Shah, a dear friend and cousin, has brought together a wealth of wisdom in these pages—wisdom born not of grand theories but of simple truths and personal experiences. His approach to business and life is refreshingly practical, and it shines through in this book with clarity and purpose.

What makes this work stand out is its unpretentious honesty. Shrenik has always believed in keeping things simple, never overcomplicating what should remain clear. His ideas are rooted in his everyday experiences—hard-earned lessons from years of dedication, persistence, and an unshakable belief in human potential. As a reader, you are not just presented with concepts, but you are taken through real-life scenarios that offer a window into the challenges and triumphs of business and personal growth.

The case studies Shrenik has included here are not just stories; they are roadmaps—guiding us toward better decision-making, improved relationships, and ultimately, more fulfilled lives. His words resonate with a deep understanding of the realities we all face, making the book not just informative but inspiring.

This book, much like Shrenik himself, offers practical wisdom wrapped in simplicity. It is a work that will surely leave a mark on its readers, as it has on me. I feel privileged to introduce it and hope that you, too, will find in its pages the same blend of insight and motivation that I did.

With warmth and admiration,

– Bhavin Shah
CEO & Director EducationWorld
MD, Access USA Associate School
Strategic Advisor, Boarding School Association of India
Mentor – World Academy of Career Programmes

INTRODUCTION

I'm not your typical author. In fact, I've never finished reading a book myself, let alone written one. The closest I've come was starting a Robin Sharma book, only to put it down halfway through. So, writing this book? It's been quite the leap of faith.

But here's how it all began. Every Sunday, I started sharing small snippets about business cases with my team and colleagues. Just practical, real-world stuff I'd learned along the way. Nothing fancy, nothing theoretical – just the nitty-gritty of business boiled down to three simple words. That's how SundayInk was born.

SundayInk is more than just a book. It's a movement born from the idea of enriching experiences and growing together. We believe passionately in the power of shared experiences in the business world. Our agenda is to make great experiences accessible, to invest a few minutes peacefully on reading and inhaling experience every Sunday.

At first, it was just for my team. But then, something unexpected happened. Friends started asking about these snippets. Startup founders began reaching out, saying they found these bite-sized, practical insights incredibly useful. The audience grew, and suddenly, I realized we might be onto something. SundayInk began welcoming people from every discipline and culture who seek a deeper understanding in specialized zones.

This book isn't meant to be a textbook or a grand theory of business. It's a practical handbook, born from the trenches of real business experiences. Each chapter is like one of those Sunday snippets – concise, practical, and hopefully, relatable. It's a treasure box of knowledge culminating from experiences, offering a "worm's eye view" on multiple aspects affecting business.

That's the beauty of it – this book is designed to spark thoughts and inspire action, no matter where you are in your business journey. It brings new and innovative solutions to the table, different business rules and theories that can be game-changers, and unique perspectives for growing businesses.

This book is for everyone. If you're a seasoned entrepreneur, you'll find new angles to consider. If you're just starting out, you'll get a head start on avoiding common pitfalls. And if you're simply curious about the business world, you'll gain practical insights that can apply to various aspects of life.

SundayInk is your quick guide tool, ensuring knowledge that can be capitalized on for an indefinite period. So, are you ready to paint your days with experience? After all, knowledge increases by sharing, not by saving.

Happy Reading!

ACKNOWLEDGEMENT

As I reflect on the journey of bringing SundayInk: The Experiential Tour to Business, I am filled with profound gratitude for the many individuals and groups whose support and encouragement have been instrumental.

To my teachers and the school that provided a solid foundation, your guidance has been invaluable. To my family, whose unwavering support and belief have been my greatest strength—this book is as much yours as it is mine.

Gratitude goes to my friends for their encouragement and enthusiasm, and to my well-wishers for their kindness and faith in this endeavor.

Thanks to my team, colleagues, and partners.

This book, SundayInk, is not merely a collection of stories but a curated treasure trove of wisdom from diverse fields, designed to enrich your professional journey. It embodies the belief that true knowledge thrives when shared, and each chapter offers fresh perspectives, innovative solutions, and actionable insights for tackling modern business challenges.

As you dive into SundayInk, I hope it serves as a source of inspiration and a practical guide to navigating the complexities of the business world. Remember, the map to success is drawn by those who dare to share their experiences, and SundayInk is a testament to that belief.

Thank you to each of you for being part of this journey and for contributing to the realization of this book. Your support has made all the difference, and for that, I am profoundly grateful.

BUSINESS RULE

EXPERIENCE 1:
The 24/48 Rule – LEARN, LOCK & UNLOCK

Learn

I recently came across the intriguing concept of the ***"24/48 Rule"*** and was immediately fascinated by its profound implications. The essence of this ideology lies in the division of responsibility between the "24" and the "48" – a delicate balance that, when struck correctly, can unlock unparalleled business success.

The "24" represents the policy and strategy makers, nestled comfortably in the temperature-controlled headquarters, crafting the grand vision. These are the visionaries, the thinkers, the architects of the plan.

In contrast, the "48" are the ground-level executors, the field operatives who brave the harsh realities of the elements to ensure the implementation of those policies and strategies. They are the heartbeat of the organisation, the ones who transform ideas into tangible results.

Lock

Captivated by this concept, I locked it firmly in my mind, eager to explore its potential application. I knew that the true test would come when I had the opportunity to put this rule into practice.

Run your Repository on a regular basis

Unlock

That opportunity soon presented itself, and with zeal and determination, we applied the 24/48 Rule to one of our client's businesses. The results were nothing short of overwhelming – a testament to the power of this principle.

The key lies in the acknowledgement that while great strategies and tactics are essential, the execution on the field truly makes the difference. As the saying goes, ***"48 always trumps 24, whether it's sport, business, or life."***

Takeaway:

The primary takeaway from this experience is the importance of respecting and nurturing the "48" – the individuals who brave the harsh realities of the field to bring the vision to life.

<u>Positive Quote</u>

As Haeman Sunim, the renowned Buddhist teacher, once said, *"The way to get started is to quit talking and begin doing."*

Activity

When would you think of implementing the 24/48 rule in your organisation?

EXPERIENCE 2:
The Hunter and Farmer – INTERPRET, INTROSPECT & INITIATE

Interpret

In our pursuit of innovative business strategies, we stumbled upon the captivating ***"Hunter and Farmer"*** theory. This concept offers a fresh perspective on how to tackle the delicate balance between acquiring new business and nurturing existing relationships.

The "Hunter" represents the relentless pursuit of new business opportunities and the constant scouting for untapped markets and untested ventures. The "Farmer," on the other hand, embodies the art of cultivating and strengthening existing business partnerships, ensuring the steady growth and sustainability of the organisation.

Introspect

To leverage this concept effectively, we must first introspect on our own strengths and capabilities. Are we better suited to assume the role of the Hunter, constantly seeking out new frontiers? Or do our skills and inclinations align more closely with the Farmer, dedicated to the meticulous care and feeding of our current client base?

The key is to strike a strategic balance between these two archetypes, recognising that both are essential for the long-term prosperity of the business. By carefully selecting the right individual for each role, we can maximise the impact and ensure that our efforts are focused on the most pressing needs of the organisation.

RESULT – By doing so reflection of the FOCUS drive towards achieving the GOAL can be visible

Initiate

With this understanding in place, it's time to take action. Allocate the roles of Hunter and Farmer based on the unique strengths and talents of your team members. Empower the Hunters to continuously scout for new opportunities, while entrusting the Farmers with the responsibility of nurturing and strengthening existing relationships.

Takeaway:

"Realign yourself to align gain"

We firmly believe that a successful business requires both the Hunter and the Farmer, each playing a crucial role in the overall growth and sustainability of the organisation. Just as the right pair of shoes will take you to the right places, the optimal blend of these two archetypes will propel your business forward, one new client and one loyal customer at a time.

Positive Quote

As the renowned business strategist Peter Drucker once said, *"Building a good customer experience does not happen by accident. It happens by design."*

Activity

How do you encourage your team to raise concerns?

EXPERIENCE 3:
The Learning – OBSERVE, PRESERVE & SERVE

Observe

In the hustle of daily business, we often overlook a crucial practice: the conscious observation of our actions, behaviours, and responses to unexpected events. This oversight is akin to neglecting a goldmine of wisdom right beneath our feet.

Imagine conducting a **"Normal Ticking Box activity – √" at the end of each day, taking stock of the valuable lessons learned.** This simple practice can transform our daily experiences into a rich inventory of knowledge, ready to be tapped when needed most.

Every single day "Take **STOCK** of **Good Learnings**" like we do in the case of Inventory management.

Preserve

Just as a well-managed inventory ensures demand fulfilment, preserving our daily learnings enables us to meet future challenges with confidence and agility. The equation is simple: the greater the learning preserving, the higher the value enhancement.

Once remembered, always remembered.

By consciously storing these insights, we create a personal repository of wisdom. Remember, once learned and properly preserved, these lessons become a permanent part of our professional toolkit, always ready for deployment.

Serve

The true power of this Learning Inventory lies in its application. Right Learning applied at the Right Time leads to the Right Delivery, much like how efficient inventory management leads to timely sales.

Consider this:

Earning Profit = Stock conversion into Sales

Astounding Results = Self-Learning applied in daily routine

By serving our preserved wisdom at opportune moments, we transform raw experiences into refined success strategies.

Remember that *"Own Mine is Goldmine"*

Takeaway:

Self-Learning Introspection is a key that unlocks the doors to our own success. By treating our daily experiences as valuable inventory, we create a personal goldmine of wisdom, always ready to yield its riches when needed.

Positive Quote

As the renowned author and motivational speaker Zig Ziglar once said, *"Develop a passion for learning. If you do so, you will never cease to grow."*

Activity

How do you capture daily business learnings?

EXPERIENCE 4:
TRIP – ROUND, AROUND & SURROUND

Delegation of powers is a common practice. However, to ensure this delegation serves the company's best interests, we propose the TRIP paradigm:

TRIP – Trust ---- Realign ---- Inquire ---- Protect

This framework emphasises the importance of balancing trust with vigilance, regular realignment of goals, proactive inquiry into potential issues, and protective measures for the future.

Case Study: The Hidden Cost of Blind Trust

Consider this scenario: A senior authority, entrusted with significant power, misuses it to personal advantage. Company funds allocated for office interiors are illicitly diverted to finance personal home renovations. The contractor's inflated bills, encompassing both corporate and personal expenses, are approved without scrutiny.

Result: The company inadvertently foots the bill for an employee's home improvements, incurring substantial unnecessary costs.

Trust With Validation on a Frequent basis to protect from undue advantage person might be intending to earn illegitimately

Implementing TRIP

1. Trust: Begin with a foundation of trust in your team.
2. Realign: Regularly reassess and realign delegated powers with company objectives.
3. Inquire: Maintain a culture of open inquiry, where questioning unusual practices is encouraged.
4. Protect: Use insights gained to fortify the company against future misuse.

"Follow Foot Trails"

This mantra reminds us to stay vigilant, tracking the path of decisions and their consequences to ensure alignment with company interests.

Takeaway:

Trust is essential, but it must be coupled with a commitment to realignment, inquiry, and protection. By setting clear examples of accountability, we create a culture that values both trust and integrity.

<u>Positive Quote</u>

"Trust is Currency, you can't afford not to invest in it."

Activity

How often do you reassess your trust in your organisation?

EXPERIENCE 5:
Bring & Solve

Don't solve problems, bring opportunities and the problem will get solved.

Often, we have seen, that our entrepreneurial skills are wasted in aligning Our's & People's expectations.

Opportunity plays a vital role since "Oppor" stands for Opportunities "Tu" for turns & "Unity": brings unity i.e. "Opportunity turns mindset and brings unity".

I am sure many must have experienced behavioural change just before the science project in our school days, annual function in college days and pre-appraisal period in our early job tenure. All of a sudden, we become more responsible and mature as we see an opportunity beckon us.

It is because everyone in this world is opportunistic right from childhood. So, opportunity attracts all of us like honey bees and unites us.

In my experience, I have seen 2 live case examples where an entrepreneur spent a lot of his time aligning peoples' expectations and 1 big opportunity just came in and things fell automatically into place

Takeaway: Leaders should Invest time in seeking opportunities and rest will follow with less effort.

Positive Quote

"Opportunity is Best Captain of all endeavour" – by SOPHOCLES

Activity

Am I prioritising problems over opportunities?

EXPERIENCE 6:
The People Profit – RETAIN, ATTAIN & SUSTAIN

The Retention Puzzle and how do you solve it?

Many businesses struggle with employee retention, often focusing on obvious factors:

- Salary Hikes
- Designation Uplifts
- Better Prospects

However, the transformation of work into a socio-economic endeavour has mandated a serious change in employee retention strategies.

The New Retention Factors

In light of changing dynamics and approaches to life satisfaction, the key factors are now:

1. Balanced Work-Life Cycle

2. Positive Work Culture

3. Organisational Transparency

ACTION: Redefining the Budget

Companies must reconsider their budget-making exercise to gain trust and improve work quality:

Old Definition: Budget = Turnover + Gross Profit + Net Profit (focus on tangibles) – New Definition: Budget = Investment in People Quality (focus on intangibles)

Our experience suggests a swift change in business outlook:

From "Actual Profit" to "People Profit"

Result

The retention of the right talent at the right time is the untold story behind profit growth.

Takeaway:

Evolve employee programmes to revolve around people's profit. This shift in focus can lead to improved retention and, consequently, sustained business growth.

<u>Positive Quote</u>

"RETAIN is Key to ATTAIN Profit"

Activity

How do you go beyond salary to retain employees?

EXPERIENCE 7:
Bilateral Negotiations – PERCEIVE, BELIEVE, RECEIVE

I really want to chat about something we all do but might not always be great at negotiations. Or as we like to call it, negotiations. It's all about how to bargain and get the best deal.

More Than Just Talking

Usually, when we think of negotiations, we picture two people talking. But it's way more than that. It's about understanding what's really going on under the surface.

In our experiences, we interpret **"Bilateral" to be "Nerves & Needs"** at the time of nEgotiations. Try to absorb & follow the equation while in the process of nEgotiations

Nerves + Needs - Ego = Effective Negotiations

Let's break that down:

Nerves – Observe the Behavioural Traits of the Opposite Person

Needs – Assess the Real Need on a deal

Ego – Downturn Ego to Upturn Deal

Why It Works

When you focus on understanding the other person and what they need, instead of just trying to "win," magic happens. Deals get done faster and everyone's happier.

"Art of Negotiations is an Arch of Deal"

This means good negotiating skills can help you build great business relationships.

Business Learning: Negotiations

Think of negotiations as a way to grow your business. It's not about tricking anyone – it's about finding a way for everyone to win.

Why It Matters

Good negotiation skills can open doors, save money, and help your business thrive.

Positive Quote

"Plug the mindset to plug the deal"

Activity

How do you manage your ego during negotiations?

EXPERIENCE 8:
Compromise Negotiations – DO, DID & DECIDE

This is about a special kind of negotiation: the compromise. Here's an equation to think about:

Compromise = (Today) Loss + Time factor - Ego = Profitable Deal (Tomorrow)

Sounds weird, right? Let's break it down.

Making or Breaking a Deal

Sometimes, you're in a situation where the deal could go either way. To tip things in your favour, try these tricks:

1. Use positive business talk: Say things like "well-choreographed" or "mending fences"
2. Be good at understanding what people really mean
3. Have a deal-making attitude
4. Be ready to compromise

Business Learning: Compromise

Here's a fun exercise: Think about your past deals. For each one, ask yourself:

1. Do: Was it a win or a loss?
2. Did: Did you compromise? Yes, or No?
3. Decide: Would you compromise again? Yes, or No?

This helps you see how compromise affects your deals over time.

"Reflect Your Experience with Yourself"

Why It Matters

Sometimes, losing a little today can mean winning big tomorrow. It's all about playing the long game.

Positive Quote

"Read Underlying Line to Win the Line"

Activity

How do you weigh short-term losses against long-term gains?

EXPERIENCE 9:
Zopa & Batna Negotiations – RANGE, CHANGE, EXCHANGE

These are some fancy-sounding terms that are actually pretty simple: ***ZOPA and BATNA.*** Don't worry, they're not as complicated as they sound!

What are ZOPA and BATNA?

ZOPA stands for Zone of Potential Agreement. It's the sweet spot where both sides can make a deal.

BATNA means Best Alternative to a Negotiated Agreement. It's your backup plan if the deal falls through.

Negotiation in Action

Think about buying a car. You start with an offer, the seller counters, and you go back-and-forth. That back-and-forth? That's ZOPA in action!

Breaking It Down

- Seller's BATNA: The lowest price they'll accept
- Buyer's BATNA: The highest price they'll pay

When these two overlap, that's your ZOPA – where a deal can happen.

The Magic Formula

Here's a simple way to think about it:

Seller BATNA (+) & Buyer BATNA (-) = ZOPA Price

In other words, when the seller's lowest acceptable price meets the buyer's highest acceptable price, you've found your ZOPA.

Why It Matters

Knowing your BATNA gives you confidence. Knowing the ZOPA helps you close deals.

ZOPA is step after BATNA

<u>Positive Quote</u>

"Walk towards Your Best Price to Get Right Price"

Activity

How do you identify your best alternatives in negotiations?

EXPERIENCE 10:
Cheat Sheet Negotiations – PREP, TRAP, WRAP

Heard of something super useful? The ***negotiation cheat sheet***. Don't worry, it's not about cheating – it's about being prepared!

What's a Cheat Sheet?

Think of it as your "Dialogue Deal Preparer." It has five parts that help you get ready for any negotiation.

The Five-Part Plan

1. Identify the Best and Worst-Case Scenario – Goal Setter – Acts as Saviour to Offer, counter offer, and settlement in the middle of a deal.
2. Reason We Here – Mind maker – acts as describing the lay of the land before initiating the negotiation.
3. Accusation Audit – Eye Breaker – Ready Reckoner for possible accusation on You, Business & Proposal if any.
4. Calibrated Curiosity – Deal Killers – Raise questions which have advanced value to you & your business.
5. Intangibles – Deal Valuable – Highlight Intangibles Valuing to You.

Why It Works

Having this cheat sheet is like having a secret playbook. It helps you stay focused and confident during tough talks.

Remember This

"Cheat Sheet is Chat Box to have Chance in nEgotiation"

This means being prepared gives you a better shot at success.

Positive Quote

"Most Unlike in School is Best Like in Business – Homework"

Activity

Have you ever used our cheat sheet in negotiations?

Positive Quote

"Most Unlike in School is Best Like in Business – Homework"

Activity

Have you ever used our cheat sheet in negotiations?

BUSINESS THEORY

EXPERIENCE 11:
The "Raise Your Hand" Approach – DISCOVER, DEPLOY & DEAL

Discover

While finding innovative solutions for my business, I stumbled upon a fascinating theory that caught my attention – the ***"Raise Your Hand"*** approach. This concept, rooted in the belief that "Raised by One and Resolved by Many," presented a compelling paradigm shift in problem-solving.

Concept

The core idea is simple yet profound – unless you raise your hand, your query or concern will remain unresolved. By actively sharing your challenges with a group of knowledgeable individuals, you unlock the power of collective wisdom. The assumption is that within any close-knit community or relevant network, there exists the expertise and experience to address the problem at hand.

Deploy

This theory encourages us to proactively "deploy" our problems, queries, and concerns, leveraging the support of the crowd to find swift and effective solutions. Rather than grappling with issues in isolation, the "Raise Your Hand" approach empowers us to tap into the diverse perspectives and problem-solving skills of our peers.

"WE"

At the heart of this approach is the recognition that the collective **"WE" is far more powerful than the individual "I."**

Deal

When faced with a problem, the "Raise Your Hand" approach urges us to deal with it as if it were our own. By taking personal ownership and deliberating on solutions promptly, we not only accelerate the problem-solving process but also cultivate a sense of shared responsibility within the group.

Walk the Solution

Remember, tomorrow you might find yourself on the same path as the problem-solver. This awareness encourages us to "walk the solution" – to actively contribute to the resolution, knowing that our actions today may benefit us or our peers in the future.

"Raise to Erase"

In essence, the "Raise Your Hand" approach can be summed up as "Raise to Erase" – by actively bringing your problems to the forefront, you enable the collective to work towards erasing them, one by one.

Takeaway:

The primary takeaway from this approach is the power of engaging multiple brains to deactivate the single-brain problem. By asking the right questions and inviting diverse perspectives, we unlock solutions that may have eluded us in isolation.

Positive Quote

As the renowned author and entrepreneur James Clear once said, ***"People who have deliberately decided to become problem solvers lead better."***

Fill-in-the-Blank Activity

1. Raised by One and ________ by Many.
2. To solve a problem within a group, it's crucial to first __________ your hand.
3. You can't ________ a problem until you're asking the ________ questions.

Options: Solve | Resolved | Right | Raise

EXPERIENCE 12:
Man 2 Man Marking – PARK, MARK & SPARK

We've developed a unique monitoring strategy called *"Man-Man Marking."* This approach assigns a leader or "master" to each key business driver, ensuring focused oversight and goal achievement.

How does it work?

The Three-Step Implementation

1. Define Critical Drivers: Identify the crucial elements driving business growth and operations.
2. Assign Leadership: Match each key driver with a suitable leader or master.
3. Monitor Performance: Track outputs and outcomes to ensure business success.

Astounding Results

Implementing Man-Man Marking has yielded remarkable outcomes:

- **"No Stone Unturned"**: Comprehensive clarity on key drivers at all levels.
- Leadership Team Performance: Enhanced focus on defined responsibilities.
- Execution Team Clarity: Clear understanding of task allocation and reporting lines.
- Result: Improved control over exceptions and deviations.

"Task with proper TICK will UN-tick the possible negative tricks"

This mantra encapsulates the essence of Man-Man Marking – thorough oversight that pre-empts potential issues.

Takeaway:

Just as in sports, business success requires multiple strategies. Man-Man Marking offers a robust framework for performance management and goal achievement.

Positive Quote

"If everything seems to be going well, you obviously don't know what's going on."

Fill-in-the-Blank Activity

1. In the Man 2 Man Marking Strategy, a business key driver is a _______ to monitor performance.
2. Unlike sports, even business requires multiple _______ for successful results
3. If everything seems to be going _______, you obviously don't know what's going on.

Options: Strategies | Well | Leader

EXPERIENCE 13:
9 Box – Pen Down Experiences – READ, WRITE & LEARN

What Are Pen-Down Stories?

These are the experiences we've had, the things we've learned, and the events that have shaped us. They're like little time capsules of wisdom.

Why Stories Matter

We all love a good success story, right? But the thing is – the stories where things didn't go so well? They're often even more valuable. They're packed with lessons that can help us do better next time.

The Power of Writing It Down

When we say, ***"Pen Down,"*** we mean literally writing down your experiences. It's amazing what can come out when you start putting pen to paper (or fingers to keyboard). You might discover:

- Paths you've taken that you'd forgotten about
- How your goals have changed over time
- New ways of looking at yourself and your work
- How different parts of your life and work connect
- Strengths you didn't know you had

Looking Back to Move Forward

When the year ends, try this: Write down your stories from the past year. Don't worry if they're good or bad – just get them down. This exercise can help you:

1. See where you've been
2. Understand where you're going
3. Figure out how to do things better next time
4. Appreciate how much you've grown

Remember: ***"Dive into the PAST to have depth in the future."***

In other words, understanding where you've been can help you go further tomorrow.

Positive Quote

"Inspiration by Yourself – Unfold folded stories within you."

Fill-in-the-Blank Activity

1. Dive into _______ to have depth in the future.
2. We tend to remember success stories, but stories with __________ often offer deeper lessons.
3. The Pen Down approach helps in reflecting on __________ for future growth.

Options: Failures | Past | Past experiences

EXPERIENCE 14:
9 Box – Best Plan Model – STRIVE, THRIVE & SURVIVE

Let's talk about the ***"Best Plan Model"*** – a way to energise your business and create a solid roadmap.

The Best Plan Model: A 9-Step Approach

1. Pen Down Stories: Remember what we talked about last time? Write down your experiences.
2. Connect Collaborative Contingency: We'll focus on this today.
3. Market Growth vs Self Growth: Balance external and internal progress.
4. Budget Well: Plan your finances carefully.
5. White Paper Strategy: Outline your big ideas.
6. Execution Plan: Figure out how to make it all happen.
7. Review AB Testing: Try different approaches and see what works.
8. Result: Measure your success.
9. Mirror Yourself: Reflect on your progress and learnings.

Connecting and Collaborating to Beat Contingencies

Here's a thought: We can't plan for everything, but we can plan to connect and collaborate better. This can help us handle unexpected situations.

Try this:

1. List possible scenarios that might happen in your business.
2. Think about how you might handle each one.
3. Consider who you could connect with or partner with within each case.

The idea is that good connections (C1) plus strong collaborations (C2) are more powerful than unexpected problems (C3). In math terms:

(C1 + C2) > C3

What Does This Mean?

- Connect: Build a strong network
- Collaborate: Find business partners
- Contingency: Be ready for unexpected situations

Result – In tough times, connection and collaboration will work as saviour to the situation

Positive Quote

"Cure Contingency while connecting collaborative Dots."

Fill-in-the-Blank Activity

1. Planning well today ensures you're ___________ for tomorrow.
2. Contingency is unplanned, but we can ______ well and engage in collaborations to mitigate it.
3. The formula (Connect C1 + Collaboration C2) > Contingency C3 suggests that _________ and collaboration can overcome challenges.

Options: Plan | connection | Prepared

EXPERIENCE 15:
9 Box – Growth Beneath the Best Plan Model – PROCEED, LEAD & SUCCEED

Looking Beyond Year-Over-Year Growth

We all believe that we tend to assess the growth YOY to understand self-performance, growth driver and best product /services of the preceding year

Market Growth vs. Company Growth

Here's the deal: It's not just about how much we've grown. We need to look at how the whole market is doing too. This gives us a better picture of how well we're really performing.

What is Market Growth?

Market growth is like taking the temperature of your entire industry. It tells you if things are heating up or cooling down for everyone, not just your company.

Think of your company's growth as Self Growth (SG). Now, here's the smart part: We want to compare this to Market Growth (MG). It's like this:

Positive Outlook – SG >= MG

If SG is greater than or equal to MG, you're doing great!

Why This Matters

Understanding market growth helps you:

1. See where you stand in your industry
2. Figure out if you're really growing or just riding a wave
3. Make better plans for the future

Remember: ***"SCAN Well to Visualise IMAGE Well"***

In other words, look closely at the market to get a clear picture of where you stand.

The Bottom Line

How the market behaves often decides how individual companies behave. It's like knowing the weather before you plan a picnic.

Positive Quote

"Know the Stadium & Pitch, before the match starts."

Fill-in-the-Blank Activity

1. Assessing _________ growth against _________ growth helps determine your company's true performance."
2. Know the _________ & Pitch before the match starts.
3. "_________ well to Visualise _________ well."

Options: Stadium | Self; market |Scan; Image

EXPERIENCE 16:
9 Box – Budget Well Best Plan Model – PLAN, DESIGN & ASSIGN

Rethinking Budgets

You know, that thing we usually rush through at the end or start of the year? Well, it's time to give it the attention it deserves.

Why Budgets Matter

Budgets aren't just about ticking boxes or crunching numbers. They're about planning your future. A good budget can be your roadmap to success.

Four Steps to Budget Well

1. Classify Well: Decide where you want to be – bold, aggressive, or conservative this year.
2. Consult Well: Get feedback from your team and even outside experts. Two heads (or more) are better than one!
3. Cover Well: Make sure your budget includes all the important stuff. Don't leave anything out.
4. Change Well: Build in some wiggle room. Things change, and your budget should be able to change too.

Remember: *"Budget Well today will be Well Budget tomorrow"*

Keeping Your Budget Fresh

Here's a tip: Check your budget regularly. See what's working and what's not. This helps you stay on top of changes in the market and in your business.

The Budget Formula

Think of it this way:

Well Thought + Well Planned = Well-Prepared

In other words, put some real thought into your budget, plan it carefully, and you'll be ready for whatever comes your way.

Your budget isn't just about restricting spending. It's about empowering your business to grow and succeed.

Positive Quote

"Budget is Not Restricting, it's Empowering."

Fill-in-the-Blank Activity

1. Budget is Not _______, it's empowering.
2. A well-prepared budget allows you to __________ future scenarios effectively.
3. A well-prepared budget today will be a well-budgeted tomorrow, which emphasises the importance of _________.

Options: Planning | Visualise | Restricting

EXPERIENCE 17:
9 Box – White Paper Strategy – DIVE, DEVISE & DRIVE

What's a White Paper Strategy?

White Paper documents help align with the company's future goals and ensure the design of varied strategies that consider past trends, performance, budget, competition, and competency.

The way towards advocating the facts & rationale for enlarging the focus and focusing on a particular segment, product, geography, etc., is best suited for the different lines of business and category it belongs to.

Why Bother with a White Paper?

A White Paper helps you:

1. Focus on what's important
2. Explain why you're doing what you're doing
3. Plan for different parts of your business (products, areas, customers)

What Does it Look Like?

It's like a detailed story of your plans, with:

- Lots of explanation
- Charts and graphs
- A close look at important info

"A Journey from Empty Brain to Wise Brain"

Keep it Safe!

Remember, your White Paper is top secret! Keep it safe so others don't steal your great ideas.

"React Rightly to Write Rightly"

Your White Paper turns your thoughts into a plan for making things happen.

Positive Quote

"Strategy is a pattern in a stream of decisions."

Fill-in-the-Blank Activity

1. A White Paper Strategy is a journey from an empty brain to a __________ brain.
2. A ________ strategy provides a clear roadmap for achieving long-term goals.
3. A White Paper Strategy is a document that reflects past trends, performance, budget, competition, and ________.
4. React Rightly to ________ rightly.

Options: Competency | White Paper | Write | Wise

EXPERIENCE 18:
9 Box – AB Testing – STICK, PEAK & TWEAK

From Plan to Action

Remember that White Paper Strategy we talked about? Well, now it's time to put it into action. But before we do, there's a smart step we should take: ***AB Testing.***

What's AB Testing?

AB Testing is like trying on two different outfits before a big event. You want to see which one looks best before you commit.

Why Bother with AB Testing?

It helps you:

1. See how your plan might work in real life
2. Get feedback from others
3. Spot problems before they happen

How Does it Work?

You create two versions of your plan (A and B) and see which one people like better. The one with the most fans is usually the winner.

Mirror to strategy is AB Testing and test to be conducted for acceptability at the opposite party, like

Employee – Wellness Programme Voting

Clients – Feedback pattern voting

Budget – Well Plan budget voting & so on

Remember: ***"Knowing gaps in advance will fill gaps for the future."***

AB Testing helps you fine-tune your strategy. It's like a mirror that shows you what your plan really looks like to others.

Result – Change – over of strategy considering the viewpoints via AB testing will help to nurture a better execution plan & better results

Positive Quote

"Know potholes before starting to walk on the road."

Fill-in-the-Blank Activity

1. AB Testing involves trying out different _______ to understand which strategy is more effective.
2. It is important to know the _______ in advance to fill gaps for the future
3. AB Testing is a realistic perspective on strategy framed and making it turn to be _________.

Options: effective | Gaps | Options

EXPERIENCE 19:
9 Box – Result – PICK, SLICK & TICK

We've come a long way with our Best Plan Model. Now it's time for the big finish: measuring our *"results."*

What Do We Mean by Results?

Results aren't just about whether we hit our targets. They're about understanding our whole journey and learning from it.

"We all eye on result which otherwise result is an eye."

This means results don't just show us how we did – they show us what to do next.

Breaking Down Results

Let's look at what makes up our results:

R – Retrospective changes: What changed along the way?

E – Estimation Effectiveness: How good were our guesses?

S – Scenarios Faced: What situations did we deal with?

U – Unified approach: Did we work well together?

L – Logics Prevailed: Did our thinking make sense?

T – Target achieved: Did we reach our goals?

The result, in a broader sense, is a runway to take off next year.

The Cycle Continues

Once we have our results, we start planning for next year. It's like a big circle that keeps going, but it's always a bit different each time around.

Positive Quote

"Walk on the Start to Talk on Result"

Fill-in-the-Blank Activity

1. The phrase "We all eye on result which otherwise result is an _______" emphasises the importance of results.

2. The result is the outcome of the steps performed during the ____________.

3. Walk on the Start to Talk on _____

Options: Result | Eye | Journey

BUSINESS CONCEPT

EXPERIENCE 20:
Curating the C.A.R.E. Model – CURATE, RATE & REITERATE

Curate

Have you ever evaluated the immense value of intangible assets? Those elusive yet powerful elements often forge the core of a company's competitive edge. Intrigued, we discovered the transformative ***C.A.R.E. model***, which offers a framework for harnessing these intangible assets to drive sustainable growth.

The C.A.R.E. model centres around three key pillars:

C – Caring for your Clients and Employees

A – Focusing on Actions

R – Ensuring Prompt Responses

E – Elevating Earnings

Rate

To truly unlock the potential of the C.A.R.E. model, we must first assess our current standing. By carefully rating our performance across each of these pillars, we can identify areas for improvement and nurture a culture of "Smart C.A.R.E." within the organisation.

This process may involve designing targeted engagement programmes and performance.

Scorecards that align with the unique strengths and focus areas of the business.

Reiterate

The journey of cultivating intangible value is an ongoing one, requiring constant vigilance and adaptation. As the business landscape evolves, we must continually re-evaluate our C.A.R.E. model, ensuring that it remains responsive to the changing needs of our clients, employees, and the market at large.

This "preach for practice" approach, which we refer to as a "continuous monogram," is essential for maintaining the desired results and positioning the organisation for long-term success. By making "SPARE YOUR TIME TO CARE" a guiding principle, we can make way for the true power of intangible assets and transform them into a formidable competitive advantage.

Takeaway:

We firmly believe that every business, regardless of its industry or size, must prioritise the value of intangibles. These elements are the seeds that will ultimately bear the fruits of tangible growth and profitability.

Positive Quote

As the renowned philosopher Kahlil Gibran once said, ***"Intangible is the real power of the universe as it is the seed of the tangible."***

Activity

Question: What does the "CARE" model emphasise in a business context?

- A) Client engagement and employee satisfaction.
- B) Increasing revenue through product innovation.
- C) Expanding market share through aggressive marketing.
- D) Minimising operational costs.

Answer: ___________

EXPERIENCE 21:
The T.A.T.K.A.L. Cell – FRAME, AIM & TRAIN

Frame

Heard of "*TATKAL*" booking for travel? It's essential to recognise the pressing need for a dedicated unit capable of addressing challenges with lightning-fast efficiency. That's what I call the T.A.T.K.A.L. Cell – a transformative framework designed to help organisations navigate even the most daunting situational hurdles.

The T.A.T.K.A.L. Cell comprises six essential elements:

T – Trim Your Thoughts

A – Activate the Clock (24/7)

T – Leverage Team Support

K – Kick Off Decisive Actions

A – Accept the Outcome

L – Embrace Continuous Learning

Aim

The primary aim of the T.A.T.K.A.L. Cell is to maximise results by minimising the time it takes to address problems. Rather than allowing issues to fester and grow, this rapid response unit is designed to tackle challenges head-on, ensuring that no opportunity for progress is lost.

Train

To harness the full power of the T.A.T.K.A.L. Cell, we must train our minds to work in sync with its underlying principles. This means cultivating the agility to "Trim Your Thoughts," the discipline to "Activate the Clock 24/7," and the courage to "Accept the Outcome" – no matter how daunting the circumstances may be.

Takeaway:

The T.A.T.K.A.L. Cell is akin to a "Tatkal Ticket" for your business – a means of transcending the limitations of "No Ticket" scenarios and seizing opportunities that may have otherwise slipped through the cracks.

Positive Quote

As the renowned business strategist Jim Rohn once said, ***"It's not about making the right decision. It's about taking a decision and making it right."***

Activity

Question: What is the primary purpose of establishing a "TATKAL Cell" within an organisation?

- A) To streamline financial reporting processes.
- B) To address and solve business problems instantly.
- C) To improve customer relationship management.
- D) To manage long-term strategic planning.

Answer:_________

EXPERIENCE 22:
The Network – TRACE, PLACE & FACE

How do you decode NETWORK?

In today's business landscape, 'network' carries a dual significance:

1. Net + Work: The ability to work from anywhere, powered by technology and Wi-Fi.

2. Net * Work: The multiplicative effect of effective networking on business growth.

Both interpretations are essential and measurable assets in today's business world.

The Network-Cashflow Paradigm

While positive cash flow indicates a company's stability, a strong network signifies its capacity for growth. This creates a new paradigm for business evaluation:

-   If cash flow is positive, the company is doing great & stable
-   If the Network is strong, the company has the Capacity to Grow

ACTION: Building a Positive Network

To harness the power of networking, follow these steps:

1. Assess Potential Network
2. Build Network
3. Explore Network

Our experience confirms that in today's business environment:

NETWORK = BUSINESS INFLUENCER = END RESULT

"Run Network which doesn't have run time error in downloading"

Takeaway:

Just as mobile networks require continuous upgrades, business networks need a '5G plan' with unlimited connections. Constant cultivation and expansion of your network are crucial for sustained business growth.

<u>Positive Quote</u>

"Network is Net Worth – connecting people to people, ideas & opportunities."

Activity

Question: What is the primary focus when assessing the strength of a business network?

- A) Network speed and bandwidth.
- B) The capacity to grow and influence the business.
- C) The number of employees connected to the network.
- D) The security protocols in place.

Answer: _______

EXPERIENCE 23:
The Freedom Paradigm – SET, LET & MET

Do you have Business Freedom?

In our experience, true business freedom can be encapsulated in the *"FREEDOM"* paradigm:

F – Follow Ethical Business Principles

R – Responsibly Set Your Own Business Rules

E – Enact Market Changes in Your Business

E – Examine Business Plan vs. Current Reality

D – Develop & Re-strategise Actions to Meet Targets

O – Organise Unstructured People, Processes & Technology

M – Maintain Focus on Your Mission

ACTION: Implementing the FREEDOM Paradigm

1. Visualise and apply this concept to transform your business results.
2. Draw inspiration from the changes observed in the last 78 years of national independence, connecting these lessons to your business strategy.

"See Wealth Within to Earn Wealth"

This encourages businesses to recognise and leverage their inherent strengths and resources.

Result

Just as the "Har Ghar Tiranga" campaign created a powerful recall value, the FREEDOM paradigm can instil a lasting impact on business learning and strategy.

Takeaway:

The Business Freedom Concept is a powerful tool for creating a strong, independent business fiefdom.

Positive Quote

"Freedom is Independence if exercised wisely."

Activity

Question: Which of the following is NOT part of the "Biz Freedom Concept"?

- A) Follow Ethical Business Principles.
- B) Set Your Own Business Rules.
- C) Focus exclusively on short-term profits.
- D) Organise unorganised people, processes, and technology.

Answer: _______

EXPERIENCE 24:
The Power – PURE, CURE & ENSURE

As we explore the concept of *power* in organisations, power, a complex and often misunderstood force, shapes the dynamics of every workplace.

Let's go into its nuances and discover how to wield it wisely.

The Essence of Power

Power isn't just about authority; it's about responsibility and influence. Interestingly, as responsibilities increase, so does one's power. This concept permits all levels of an organisation, from the admin team to directors and stakeholders.

Let's break down power into its core components:

P – Perform: Deliver results consistently

O – Orator: Communicate effectively

W – Act Wisely: Make judicious decisions

E – Enact Ideas & Suggestions: Bring thoughts to life

R – Reprimand Rarely: Guide more, criticise less

The Wise Use of Power

The key lies not in having power but in using it judiciously. As the saying goes, "Don't sleep with the pillow of Power." It's a reminder that power should be a tool for positive change, not a comfort to rest upon.

Action Steps:

1. Conduct a "Position Power Mapping Activity" to visualise power distribution within your organisation.
2. Assess and monitor the intrinsic values associated with each level of authority.
3. Focus on developing the underlying aspects of power rather than pursuing power for its own sake.

Power isn't just about position. It's about how you perform, communicate, make decisions, implement ideas, and guide others. True power lies in the ability to inspire and lead, not just to direct.

Takeaway:

To hold power effectively, one must first respect it. Understanding the responsibilities that come with power is crucial for ethical and effective leadership.

<u>Positive Quote</u>

"It Takes Time or Does Time Take it?"

Activity

Question: How should power be exercised within an organisation, according to the blog?

- A) By centralising all decision-making authority.
- B) By using it sparingly and with wisdom.
- C) By delegating it indiscriminately across all levels.
- D) By avoiding responsibility to increase personal power.

Answer: _______

EXPERIENCE 25:
Biz Festival – ENLIGHT, DELIGHT & BRIGHT

On this occasion, the identification of Business Happiness (Triple S) with a magnifying glass should be done at the holistic level. It can even be construed as

- Sense of Success & Gratitude Week
- Sense of Satisfaction
- Sense of Smile on Face

We'll agree that Triple "S" will defer and invariably be person to person. Hence, the concept of EBITA should be explored in "intangible form" over & above the tangible form of profit

- Identifying & Sharing Success & Gratitude – Increases Motivation Productivity
- Measuring Satisfaction – Get to draw Roadmap – Actual Result
- Bringing Smile – Relationship – Long-Term Gain

"Normal Smile + Satisfaction + Success = Big SMILE"

ACTION

We have experienced a Sense of Gratitude Inverse Theory being implemented as it's difficult to remember & acknowledge the efforts of someone without any expectations.

Further, generate & display Positivity to create a sense of satisfaction & smile.

Result – In our view, we should "work on 'Wealth of Happiness' to have actual Wealth in turn."

Takeaway:

The chain of "Triple S" will change the dynamics of business.

Positive Quote

"Better to Share than to Hold"

Activity

Question: What does the "Triple S" in business happiness represent?

- A) Success, Satisfaction, Smile.
- B) Strategy, Strength, Security.
- C) Sales, Services, Supply.
- D) Structure, Systems, Sustainability.

Answer: ______

EXPERIENCE 26:
Cube Intro – FOLD, BOLD & UNFOLD

What's the Cube Intro?

Starting a new job can be nerve-wracking, right? That's where the "***Cube Intro***" comes in. It's a new way of introducing people to their job that goes beyond the usual "here's your desk" approach.

Why "Cube"? Well, it's got three sides to it:

1. Getting to know your department
2. Understanding your job
3. Meeting your coworkers (and this is where it gets interesting!)

The Third Side of the Cube

Usually, when you start a new job, you learn about what you'll be doing and who the important people are. But the Cube Intro adds something extra – it tells you a bit about your coworkers' personalities.

"Way towards Nervous New to Confident NEW"

Why does this matter? Well, it helps in a few ways:

—   You get to know your team better, faster
—   You understand how people think
—   You know what people expect from you

A Real-Life Example

We recently tried this with a senior person who joined our company. Here's what happened:

—   They felt at home right away
—   They were confident from day one
—   It felt more like joining a family than just a company

The Cube Intro is all about turning nervous newbies into confident team members. It's about making people feel comfortable and ready to contribute from the get-go.

Positive Quote

"Turn The Table to Turn the People."

Activity

Question: What is the unique aspect of the "Cube Intro" method mentioned in the blog?

- A) It focuses solely on technical skills.
- B) It introduces new employees to the behavioural traits of colleagues.
- C) It excludes any personal introductions.
- D) It ignores the new employee's job profile.

Answer: ______

EXPERIENCE 27:
Competitor Dost – NERVE OBSERVE & SERVE

Remember when India helped Turkey and Syria after the earthquake? They called it "Operation Dost" (Dost means friend). It showed how countries can help each other, even if they're not always close.

What Can Businesses Learn?

Let's talk about something that might sound strange: being friends with your competitors. We call it ***"Competitor Dost."***

Why Watch Your Competitors?

We often keep an eye on our competitors to:

- Understand their strategies
- See their results
- Guess their next moves

But what if we took it a step further?

The Competitor Dost Idea

Here's a wild thought: What if we helped our competitors when they're in trouble? It sounds crazy, but it could create a healthier business world for everyone.

"Open Arms Will Close the Door of Wrong Arms."

This means that being kind to competitors can stop unfair practices in business.

Setting an Example

Just like India showed good values by helping other countries, businesses can show good values, too. It's about creating a positive business culture.

Remember: ***"Be Positive when the Competitor situation is Negative."***

By being a good "dost" to competitors, we can make the whole business world better.

<u>Positive Quote</u>

"Be in the Line to Clear the Line"

Activity

Question: What is the key takeaway from the "Competitor Dost" concept?

- A) To always outperform your competitors at any cost.
- B) To offer support to your competitors during their crises.
- C) To ignore your competitors entirely.
- D) To sabotage your competitors' strategies.

Answer: _______

EXPERIENCE 28:
Blue Collar Dost – MEET, GREET & TREAT

We generally tend to emphasise the Top & Middle level of management to be graded and rated in the organisation.

Focus is always embedding on the varied encouraging HR activities for such level of management. We generally tend to emphasise the Top & Middle level of management to be graded and rated in the organisation.

Well, today, let's talk about the unsung heroes – our ***blue-collar workers.***

Who Are Blue-Collar Workers?

These are the folks who keep things running smoothly – the ones on the factory floor, in the warehouses, or out in the field. They're a crucial part of any business, but sometimes, we forget to show them how much they matter.

Showing Some Love

What if we treated our blue-collar workers like VIPs? Here are some cool ideas:

1. Coffee with the Boss: Imagine a factory worker sharing a cup of joe with the CEO!
2. Holiday Surprises: How about a surprise trip for the hardest workers?
3. Awards and Recognition: Let's celebrate their achievements in style.
4. Respect Meter: Make sure everyone treats them with the respect they deserve.

Remember: ***"Support Blue-Collar to become White Collar."***

This means helping these workers grow, and maybe one day, they'll be running the show!

Why It Matters

When we show our blue-collar workers we care, amazing things happen. They feel part of the team and often go above and beyond in their work.

Business Learning: Blue-Collar Dost

Create a place where blue-collar workers can shine. Let them show off their skills and grow within the company.

Positive Quote

"Bow Down to Lift Up"

Activity

Question: What does the "Blue Caller Dost" concept encourage?

- A) Focus only on top and middle management.
- B) Empowering and recognising blue-collar employees.
- C) Implementing strict hierarchical structures.
- D) Limiting employee engagement to senior management.

Answer: _______

EXPERIENCE 29:
Society Dost – DEAL, SEAL & APPEAL

How can businesses help make the world a better place? You might've heard of Corporate Social Responsibility (CSR), but let's think even bigger.

What's CSR?

CSR is when big companies use some of their money to help society. It's a great start, but what if everyone got involved, not just the big guys?

A New Way to Think: **CSR – Come & Share Responsibility**

Imagine if we all chipped in to help our communities, not because a law says we have to, but because we want to. Great, right?

Small Steps, Big Impact

"Small baby steps in lieu of betterment will be elderly support to society"

This means even little things we do can make a big difference over time.

Everyone Can Help

You don't need to be a big shot to make a difference. We can all do something:

- Volunteer at a local charity
- Donate to causes we care about
- Help a neighbour in need

Business Learning: Society Dost

For businesses, think about how you can use your resources (time, money, skills) to help your community. It's not just good for society – it's good for business, too!

Why It Matters

When businesses help society, everyone wins. The community gets stronger, and the business builds a great reputation.

Positive Quote

"Business is independent with society being dependent."

Activity

Question: What is the essence of the "Society Dost" concept?

- A) Focusing solely on business profits.
- B) Allocating time and resources to benefit society.
- C) Ignoring corporate social responsibilities.
- D) Centralising all business decisions.

Answer: __________

EXPERIENCE 30:
Update Dost – FORM, PERFORM & INFORM

Let's talk about something that might sound boring but is super important: staying up-to-date with rules and regulations. Yep, we're talking about compliance.

The Compliance Challenge

We all agree that being non-compliant invites open admission to regulatory bodies to act upon and has changed the fate of multiple companies.

Be in the Know

The key is to always be aware of what's changing. New rules, guidelines, laws – they're always popping up. It's like keeping your phone's apps updated for your business.

100% is the Goal

We usually think an employee doing 80% of their job is pretty good. But when it comes to following rules, we need to aim for 100%. No shortcuts here!

"BE Alert on Update to be Awake on Non-Compliance"

This means if we stay on top of updates, we won't get caught off guard by rule changes.

Creating an Update System

Take a moment to think: Do you have a way to keep track of all the rules your company needs to follow? If not, it might be time to create one.

"Stay Connected to Stay in Touch"

Business Learning: Update Dost

Here's a thought: Following the rules isn't just about avoiding trouble. It can actually help your business do better! Think of it as scoring points for being a good corporate citizen.

Why It Matters

When your business stays up-to-date, you're always ready for whatever comes your way. No surprises, no panic.

Positive Quote

"Update Your Compliance like we update status on WhatsApp."

Activity

Question: What is the primary focus of the "Update Dost" concept?

- A) Ignoring regulatory updates to focus on core business activities.
- B) Regularly update and comply with new norms and regulations.
- C) Delegating compliance tasks to external agencies.
- D) Avoiding compliance costs to maximise profits.

Answer: _______

PROTECT YOUR BUSINESS

EXPERIENCE 31:
Whistle Blowing – FIGURE, TRIGGER & RIGOUR

Organisations must figure out robust mechanisms to safeguard their interests and maintain ethical standards. Enter the Vigil Mechanism, a powerful tool that leverages tips and whistles as key factors in protecting corporate integrity.

The essence of this approach lies in creating a Whistle Ecosystem – a safe and effective channel for employees, vendors, customers, and other stakeholders to alert the company about potential wrongdoings, mishaps, or malpractices.

Trigger

The effectiveness of a Whistle Management system hinges on adequate awareness among all connected parties. Research indicates that a staggering 41% of frauds are investigated based on triggered tips. This statistic underscores the vital importance of whistleblowing in directly protecting organisations from fraud and misconduct.

By fostering an environment where stakeholders feel empowered to speak up, companies can tap into a powerful network of vigilant observers, each capable of sounding the alarm at the first sign of impropriety.

Rigour

To truly harness the power of whistleblowing, organisations must adopt a rigorous approach to dealing with triggered tips. This means not only encouraging the reporting of potential issues but also ensuring that each report is thoroughly investigated and addressed.

Supporting these actions with a well-crafted Whistle Blow policy is crucial. Remember, it's essential to work on whistles before they fall silent – every moment of inaction is an opportunity lost in the fight against corporate malpractice.

"Your Silence will not Protect You."

Takeaway:

The power of whistleblowing lies in its anonymity. As the saying goes, "Someone is watching behind the scenes & can come on scene without face/identity." This invisible guardian serves as a constant reminder that unethical behaviour can be exposed at any moment, fostering a culture of integrity and accountability.

Positive Quote

"I'm as clean as a whistle."

To what extent have you implemented Whistleblow Technique in your organization?

EXPERIENCE 32:
The Green Flag Paradox – TENDER, RENDER & SURRENDER

What is the Green Flag?

A **"Green Flag"** represents behaviour that seems *"Too Good to Be True."* It's when an individual demonstrates kindness or generosity towards the company that goes beyond reasonable expectations. While seemingly positive, these actions can sometimes mask underlying issues or fraudulent intentions.

Setting the ALARM

Every business should establish an Early Warning Signal system to identify and register Green Flag cases. This proactive approach helps prevent the potential escalation of fraud.

Case Studies: The Many Faces of Green Flags

1. Lavish Gifts to Coworkers
2. Consistently Unclaimed Reimbursements
3. Personal Credit Card Use for Company Expenses
4. Excessive Weekend "Business" Trips

These seemingly benevolent actions may indicate deeper issues, from attempts to gain favour to hiding fraudulent activities.

The Monitoring Imperative

Creating a monitoring environment to capture such events should be a continuous process within the business architecture. Upon identifying Green Flag instances, formal discussions should ensue to understand the motivations behind such behaviours.

"Distrust the Obvious"

This principle serves as a reminder to look beyond surface-level generosity and question unusually accommodating behaviour.

Takeaway:

Cultivate awareness of unusual signs or inconsistencies, always considering behavioural traits that might indicate potential fraud. Remember, what appears as kindness may sometimes be a smokescreen for misconduct.

<u>Positive Quote</u>

"Eye the Unusualness to See Usualness in Business"

EXPERIENCE 33:
Red Flags in Business – SHAKEN, RECKON & WEAPON

Defining the Red Flag

A **Red Flag** in business is a subtle yet potent indicator that challenges fundamental principles and potentially leads into the grey area of fraud. These are circumstances that deviate from normal activity, serving as possible warning signs without definitively proving guilt or innocence.

RECKON: The Journey of Unusual Footprints

To effectively combat fraud, businesses must RECKON – Recognise and Examine circumstances knocking on normalcy. This process involves an intensive study and investigation of unusual patterns or behaviours.

Case Studies: Red Flags in Action

1. Financial Struggles: Multiple loans from colleagues
2. Lifestyle Incongruities: Sudden expensive purchases
3. Unusual Associations: Frequent, informal meetings with vendors or customers
4. Wheeler-Dealer Attitude: Constantly bending the rules or finding loopholes

The Red Flag Monitoring Mechanism: A Weapon Against Fraud

Implementing a robust Red Flag Monitoring Mechanism serves as a powerful weapon against fraudulent intentions. Our experience shows that vigilant Red Flag monitoring significantly reduces fraud penetration, filling a crucial gap in the risk environment.

"When You're Threat, You're Always a Target"

This philosophy reminds us that being aware of potential threats makes us better equipped to defend against them.

Takeaway:

Cultivate a keen eye for unusual signs or inconsistencies, always considering behavioural traits that might indicate potential fraud. Remember, the path to fraud prevention is paved with vigilance and attention to detail.

By adopting the Red Flag concept and implementing effective monitoring mechanisms, businesses can create a more secure, transparent, and ethical operational environment.

<u>Positive Quote</u>

"The greatest threat to mankind is mankind."

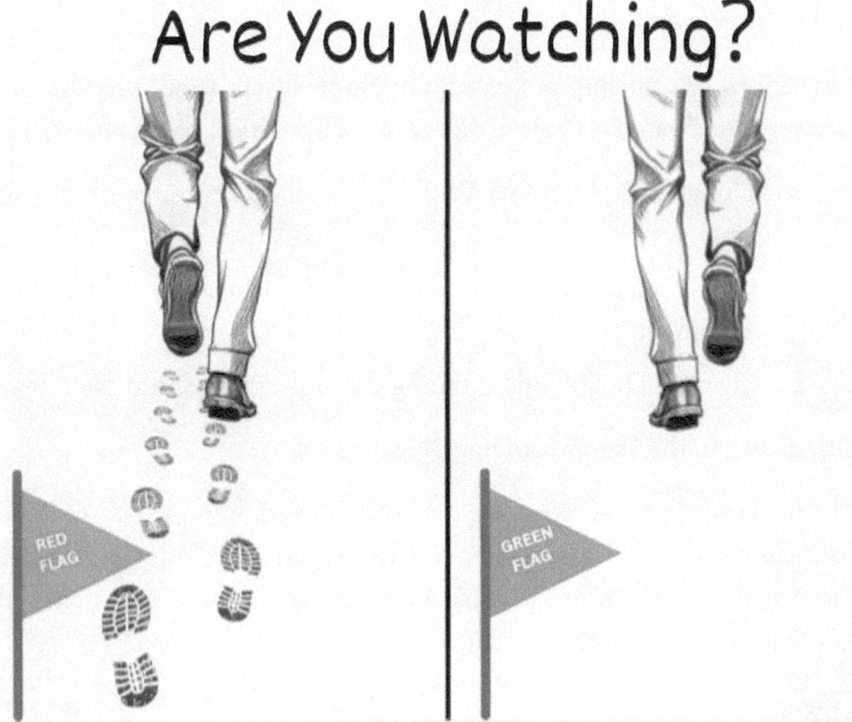

EXPERIENCE 34:
The Vendor Vigilance Triangle – REFER, PREFER & OFFER

Refer: The Overlooked Starting Point

When companies invite quotations from multiple vendors, they often overlook a crucial aspect: the origin of the vendor reference. Our experience shows that understanding "who referred whom" is a vital first step in the vendor selection process.

"Vigilance at Start will appeal Green signal at the START of Vendor Journey."

This emphasises the importance of due diligence from the very beginning of the vendor relationship.

Prefer: Implementing Logical Vigilance

After initial referencing, preference should be given based on a thorough "Background Search – Logical Vigilance." This critical phase involves:

a. Physical Visit Report: Verifying actual existence, capability, and vintage

b. Compliance & Constitution Status: Ensuring legal and regulatory alignment

c. Owner's Desk: Understanding the leadership behind the vendor

Offer: Sealing the Deal with Due Diligence

The final stage involves selecting the vendor based on proper KYC (Know Your Customer) and comprehensive information. A well-designed Vendor Assessment Form, complete with necessary documentation, marks the culmination of the vendor vigilance process.

"Vigilance at the start, Logical Vigilance in Mid & Documentary vigilance at the end = right vendors."

This equation succinctly captures the three-stage process of effective vendor selection.

Takeaway:

Maintaining a "Mystery Eye" in vendor vigilance is key to safeguarding your business interests. This approach helps mitigate risks and ensures transparency in vendor relationships.

Positive Quote

"Go off the boundaries to remain in the trade boundaries."

Have You Scanned Your Vendor?

EXPERIENCE 35:
Fraud – Debatable Moonlighting

I would like to share about ***"Fraud Debatable – Moonlighting",*** which falls under the purview of any business with multiple employee benefits.

Moonlighting – In simple words, a person undertakes a second/dual job responsibility & compromises with the original work contract with the initial employment.

This is a serious outrage that happened after COVID wherein the benefits of WFH – Work from Home were exploited by multiple individuals.

Multiple debates & arguments on whether moonlighting is fraud or unacceptable, as it encounters the possible dent in an individual's productivity.

Based on our experience in Fraud Investigation & Anti Frauds, we have come across multiple ways to identify such incidents exist within the Company if it intends to:

- BBC Test – Beyond Background Check of Employees
- RT PCR Test – Rapid Psychometric Test on Vulnerabilities
- CWIP Test – Close Watch on Individual Productivity
- VIP's Test – Visit to Individual Place of Employment on surprise
- MYC Test – Mystery Interview Call with suspected employee

"Unblink eyes to enlighten the moonlighting."

Positive Quote

"Reduce Power to Empower" – Employees Wishlist"

BUSINESS DATABASE

EXPERIENCE 36:
Data is God of Universe – PRIMACY, SECRECY & SUPREMACY

How do you treat DATA?

Data is the collection of facts and statistics gathered together for reference or analysis. Nowadays, it's most often stored in a digital format thanks to advancements in computer programmes that can store large volumes of information.

According to Forbes, 59% of businesses are using data analytics in different ways to make better decisions and increase their business performance.

Starting from marketing and sales to HR and IT, data helps business owners understand their customers, predict customer behaviour patterns, identify trends, improve the quality of services they provide, cut costs, develop new products, and more.

One of the most common reasons enterprises value data is because it helps them gain a competitive advantage over their competitors.

A famous quote by Daniel Keys Moran sums it up nicely:

"You can have data without information, but you cannot have information without data."

Here's how you treat DATA:

We emphasise on the "Look at the Next Era Generation Data", which further will be coming under "the regulatory lens of GDPR (General Data Protection Regulation) applicable in European Nations and under approval in parliament presented by Justice BN Sri Krishna Committee.

Data can be interpreted as a "conglomerate" form of information.

Positive Quote

"Who has data has power."

EXPERIENCE 37:
The Data Envelope – INTEGRATE, INITIATE & INNOVATE

We talked about data being like a universe. Well, now let's zoom in on something called the ***"Data Envelope."*** It's a fancy term, but don't worry – we'll break it down into bite-sized pieces.

The Data Envelope is all about three key things:

1. Data Relevancy
2. Data Mining Capability
3. Data Analysis Math

Let's take a closer look at each one:

1. Data Relevancy: Finding the Right Stuff

Imagine you're looking for a needle in a haystack. That's kind of what it's like when you're trying to find the right information in a sea of data. The key is to be smart about what you're looking for. Remember: *"To be rightful & thoughtful."*

2. Data Mining: Digging for Gold

Data mining is like being a detective. You're looking for patterns and trends in all that information. The trick is to have access to good market data. As they say, *"Aware is better than unaware."*

3. Data Analysis Math: Crunching the Numbers

Once you've got your data, you need to make sense of it. That's where math comes in. Don't worry – you don't need to be a math genius. Just follow the right steps, and you'll get there. Remember: *"Follow the Process of Analysis to secure results."*

Putting It All Together

When you combine these three things – relevancy, mining, and analysis – you create what we call a "Data Envelope." It's like a package that helps keep your data organised and useful.

As one wise person said: ***"Create a Rhythm Envelope to have data in rhythm."***

Taking Action

Now, here's the important part: data isn't just something that sits on the sidelines. To really make it work for you, you need to take action. Use the right data, mine it effectively, and analyse it properly. When you do this, you'll start to see things in a whole new light.

Takeaway:

Keep working on your Data Envelope. It's not a one-time thing – it's something you need to maintain and improve over time. If you do, you'll see your company's performance get better and better.

<u>Positive Quote</u>

"Data are sums of stories & pick few stories to make it meaningful."

EXPERIENCE 38:
Data Security – PRESERVE, PROTECT & PRIORITISE

Data security is the practice of protecting digital information from unauthorised access, corruption, or theft throughout its entire lifecycle. As data is being traversed, there is a chance of misuse.

Think of it this way: ***"Data without security is like a car without a seatbelt."*** You wouldn't drive without buckling up, right? The same goes for your data.

The Threat of Cybercrime

Now, you might be wondering, "Who would want to steal my data?" Well, there's a whole world of cybercrime out there.

Here's a scary fact: In just the first three months of 2022, India saw 18 million cyber-attacks. That's about 200,000 attacks every single day! It's like a non-stop digital battle out there.

Protecting Your Data

So, what can we do about it? Here are a few tips:

Look for "open windows": Just like you'd check your house for unlocked doors or open windows, check your digital world for weak spots.

Train your team: Make sure everyone in your company knows about common cyber tricks. Things like:

- Phishing emails (those sneaky emails trying to steal your info)
- Fake bank account change notices
- OTP (One-Time Password) scams
- Hackers trying to break into your systems

Keep learning: The digital world changes fast, so keep up with new security tricks.

Positive Quote

"Security should be built in, not bolt-on."

EXPERIENCE 39:
Data Mining – SELECTION, EXPLORATION & CLASSIFICATION

What's Data Mining All About?

Data mining is easier to understand if you imagine the process of mining valuable earth resources like gold or diamonds. Just like in mining for minerals, the goal of data mining is to extract the most valuable pieces of information from outstandingly large data sets.

Before You Start Digging

Before you grab your digital shovel, there are a few things to consider:

1. What's your goal? Know what you're looking for.
2. What results do you want? Have a clear picture of what success looks like.
3. How big is your data, and can your tech handle it?
4. Is your team up to the task?
5. How good are you at spotting patterns and making sense of what you find?

Why Bother with Data Mining?

Data mining is powerful stuff. It can help you:

- Predict what might happen in the future
- Understand what's happening right now

"Data mining is a tool to transform the data universe into a data planet."

In other words, it takes all that overwhelming information out there and turns it into something you can actually use.

Here's a thought to chew on:

"Without big data analytics, companies are blind and deaf, wandering out onto the web like deer on a freeway."

Scary, right? But true. In today's digital world, if you're not using your data, you're missing out big time.

Positive Quote

"Data will talk to you if you're willing to listen."

EXPERIENCE 40:
Data Back-Up – CORE, STORE & RESTORE

Data backup is like your emergency plan. It's like having a spare tyre in your car – you hope you never need it, but you're really glad it's there when you do.

Why Do We Need Backups?

Life happens, and sometimes things go wrong. Here are some situations where you'll be thankful for a good backup:

Simple Analogy on Data Backup Need arises when:

- Sudden Drip of System
- Contingency Event
- Shift of Location
- Change Management
- Cyber Attack

It's not just about big companies, either. Backing up is important for everyone, everywhere. It helps you:

- Timely Recovery
- Prompt support to Customers
- Avoid Operations Shutdown
- BCP Plan – Business Continuity

Here's something to think about: ***"Backup failure or incomplete backup is like being in the hospital without health insurance."***

You definitely don't want to be in that situation.

What Can You Do?

There are lots of ways to back up your data. You might want to look into:

- Real-time backups (that happen as you work)
- Disaster recovery plans (for worst-case scenarios)
- Good old-fashioned hard drive backups

Remember to think about all your systems – your computer's operating system, your money stuff, and any other important work systems.

<u>Positive Quote</u>

"Backup really is Frontend as Data Saviour."

Activity

Database Checklist

- ☐ **Ensure Accurate Data Entry & Storage:** Secure access and use of digital systems.

- ☐ **Maintain Data Relevancy:** Filter, categorise, and align data with objectives.

- ☐ **Implement Data Security:** Protect against threats and train employees regularly.

- ☐ **Establish Reliable Backups:** Regularly test and secure backup systems.

- ☐ **Conduct Effective Data Analysis:** Apply methods for better decision-making.

- ☐ **Comply with Regulations:** Follow legal standards and update compliance regularly.

- ☐ **Use Clear Data Visualisation:** Continuously improve visualisation techniques.

- ☐ **Commit to Continuous Improvement:** Regularly enhance data management practices.

- ☐ **Monitor Data Quality:** Regularly review and clean data to ensure accuracy and consistency.

- ☐ **Facilitate Data Integration:** Ensure smooth integration of data across different systems and platforms.

BUSINESS STRENGTH

EXPERIENCE 41:
ART Budget – OBJECT, PROJECT & INJECT

When it comes to business projection, this rule applies to most successful business decisions from my personal experience.

Object: Every year, the company shall Narrate its Future Objects and expects the Others To follow on it.

Generally, we have observed the company frames the objectives, and while sharing with the team, the message of "WE OBJECT" gets louder without words. We tend to enter into the discussion with few leaders and expect the acceptance largely.

Project: – To respect the object with the company's stands the projection suiting best to all gets announced.

We all admit the projections are based primarily on maths and the history/ trends the company has performed, and accordingly, with the help of experts, the budget/projections are finalised and announced as FUTURE PLAN.

Inject: Instead of ONLY Maths, ADD Science TO Budget

Inject means adding something impactful, and it is strongly suggested to add science in budget preparation, meaning ART Budget, as we have experienced for one of our clients, which had an astounding result with growth of 55% based on ART.

A – Action R – Reaction T – Target

ART Budget covers multiple level budgets with science, attracting the team to accept with positivity and explores the best potential of a team within the company, which justifies the reason for looking for additional growth (normal growth rate 10-20% & ART Budget 50% above)

"ART is TO APPLY ART BUDGET"

Takeaway:

Beyond Maths and Beyond Me is the time to look for an ART Budget, where science works with the concept of WE DREAM instead of ME dream.

<u>Positive Quote</u>

"The Budget is just not numbers but an expression of our values and aspirations."

EXPERIENCE 42:
The Art of Budget Creation – ATTACH, ABSORB & APPEAL

Budgets. Usually, they're something only the top folks in a company deal with. But what if we changed that?

Attach: Getting Everyone on Board

Here's an idea: What if we shared the budget with everyone in the company? It's like saying, "Hey, team, we're all in this together!" When everyone knows the plan, they can help make it happen.

Absorb: Making the Budget Real

Knowing the budget is one thing but figuring out how to make it happen is another. Instead of the bosses telling everyone what to do, why not ask the team for ideas? They might know some tricks the higher-ups haven't thought of!

Appeal: Leaders Showing the Way

You know what really gets people moving? Seeing the boss roll up their sleeves and get to work. When leaders show they're serious about the budget, everyone else follows along.

Remember: *"Actions = No Time --- Reactions = With Time ---- Target – ON time"*

This means: If we act now, we don't waste time. If we wait and react, we lose time. But if we do it right, we hit our target on time!

A budget that stays on paper doesn't do much good. It's when we put it into action that it really shines.

Positive Quote

"ODDs coming together will make the situation EVEN."

EXPERIENCE 43:
Know Your Customer – TIP, TAP & TOP

Beyond KYC:

While KYC is a familiar term in business, its importance has evolved significantly. Today, it's not just about onboarding; it's about continuous customer engagement.

The New Customer Dynamics

In light of changing customer expectations, key factors now include:

1. Depth of Customer Connection
2. Frequency of Customer Interactions
3. Insights into Customer Development

"Engage Your Customer instead of only KNOW Your Customer"

This mantra encapsulates the shift from static knowledge to dynamic engagement.

ACTION: The Unique Reality Check

We've experienced positive outcomes by conducting a Unique Reality Check with existing clients. This approach:

- Encourages honest feedback
- Excites customers to share insights on multiple parameters
- Tailors the engagement to respective needs

We firmly believe that customers are the backbone of business. Ensuring the "fitness of customers to stay healthy in your business" is crucial.

Result

To gauge the modality of clients, engage with them consistently and meaningfully.

Takeaway:

Evolve your Customer Engagement Programmes to retain clients for the long-term. This shift from mere knowledge to active engagement can lead to stronger, more enduring business relationships.

<u>Positive Quote</u>

"Care more to reduce dare."

EXPERIENCE 44:
Know Your Competitor – TRACE, RAISE & PRAISE

In our previous edition, we explored KYC as "Know Your Customer." Now, we're shifting gears to interpret KYC as ***"Know Your Competitor."*** This quick self-assessment will help you build and implement "Competitive Intelligence" tailored to your company's needs.

Key Drivers of Competitor Intelligence:

1. Identification

    – Who are the players in your market?
    – How many competitors do you face?

2. Comprehension

    – What is your market share?
    – How does it compare to your competitors?

3. SWOT Analysis

    – What are your competitors' strengths and weaknesses?
    – What opportunities and threats do they present?
    – How does their quality compare in the market?

The EV Analogy:

In today's world of electric vehicles, think of your competitor as a charging station for your EV business. They provide the energy that drives you forward, challenging you to improve and innovate.

Action Steps:

1. Conduct a thorough evaluation of your business using the key drivers listed above.
2. Regularly update your competitor intelligence to stay informed about market dynamics.

3. Use this information to refine your strategies and improve your market position.

Result

To earn more, learn more about your competitors. Understanding their moves will help you make better decisions for your own business.

Takeaway:

Make competitor analysis a regular part of your business routine. It's not just about keeping tabs on them; it's about understanding the market landscape and your place within it.

Positive Quote

"Respect your competitors instead of trying to knock them out."

EXPERIENCE 45:
Know Your Palms – RUN, TURN & LEARN

Building on our previous explorations of "Know Your Customer" and "Know Your Competitor," we now turn our attention to ***"Know Your Palms."*** This concept invites us to delve into the numbers that define our market presence.

Surprisingly, this crucial aspect often receives less priority than it deserves.

Decoding "Know Your Palms":

- "Palms" represents your company's overall performance
- It encompasses Line of Business, geographical coverage, and market matrices
- Additional parameters can be included based on your company's unique needs
- Remember: "Palm" reversed is "Lamp" – illuminating your business landscape

The Number Game:

1. Data Mining

    - Regularly assess and evaluate your company's footprints
    - "Palms represent real footprints" in the market

2. Market Matrices

    - Analyse your share in different market segments
    - Identify trends and patterns in your performance

3. Geographical Coverage

    - Understand your strengths and weaknesses across regions
    - Spot opportunities for expansion or consolidation

Action Steps:

1. Implement regular data mining activities
2. Create a dashboard for easy visualisation of key metrics
3. Use insights to overcome shortcomings and enhance benefits

Result:

To beat the numbers, you must first learn the numbers. Understanding your market position is crucial for strategic decision-making.

Takeaway:

Monitor your "Palms" in real-time to gain a competitive edge in the market. Your numbers tell a story – make sure you're listening.

Positive Quote

"Monitor your Palms as they change undoubtedly.

EXPERIENCE 46:
Know Your Strength – UNTAP, TAP & APT

Remember how we talked about knowing your customers, competitors, and even your palms?

What's Your Strength All About?

When we say, ***"Know Your Strength,"*** we're not just talking about your personal biceps (though those are great, too!). We're talking about a whole range of strengths that make you and your company unique. It's like having a secret superpower for your business!

Think about it:

- Your own personal strengths
- Your company's overall mojo
- The awesome partners you work with
- The culture that makes your workplace special
- Those rock-solid documents and processes
- And, of course, your incredible team

When you put all these together, it's like assembling the Avengers of business strength!

Strength = Power

Here's a thought: When you add up all these strengths, you get something even more awesome – power! It's like combining ingredients to make the most delicious business cake ever.

Time for Action!

So, how do you tap into this power? It's all about understanding, soaking in, and amplifying the multiple strengths within your reach. Sounds fancy, right? But it's actually pretty simple:

1. Take a good look at what you're great at.

2. Appreciate the strengths of those around you.
3. Find ways to make these strengths even stronger.

We can't stress this enough – regularly check in on your "Potential Strengths Within." It's like giving your business a regular health check-up.

The Big Payoff

Here's the exciting part – when you really get to know your strengths, amazing things start happening. It's like suddenly realising you've had the key to a treasure chest all along!

Takeaway:

Knowing your strength is like being a mineral explorer, but instead of digging in the ground, you're digging within yourself and your company. There's gold in them thar hills – and those hills are you!

Positive Quote

"Multiple Strengths Will Multiply Results."

EXPERIENCE 47:
Know Your Vendors – INVOLVE, REVOLVE & EVOLVE

We've covered knowing your customers, competitors, strengths, and even your palms. Now, let's shine a spotlight on an often-overlooked superstar: your ***vendors!***

Why Vendors Matter

Vendors are not just suppliers; they're potential game-changers. Getting to know them isn't just smart—it's essential in today's fast-paced business world.

Beyond the Basics

Does knowing your vendor mean just having their contact info? Those days are long gone! Now, it's all about really understanding who they are before you even think about placing an order. It's like dating—you want to know who you're getting involved with, right?

Vendor Assessment

Here's where it gets exciting. We're not just talking about a simple background check. We're talking about a full-on vendor scan. It's like giving your potential business partners a friendly but thorough health check-up.

What's in a Vendor Scan?

- Genuineness: Are they the real deal?
- Capacity: Can they handle your needs?
- References: Who vouches for them?
- Business History: How long have they been around?
- Coverage: Where can they reach?
- Trade Cred: What do others in the industry say?
- Legal Compliance: Are they following the rules?
- Reputation: What's their street cred like?

- Physical Presence: Do they have a real address?
- KYC Compliance: Have they done their paperwork?

Why Bother?

Your vendors can make or break your business. But seriously, knowing them well is like having a secret weapon. It helps you avoid surprises (the bad kind) and builds a foundation for awesome partnerships.

"Vendor Scan at the start to have Visible Image later."

How to take action?

Don't just stop at KYC. Dive deeper! Make vendor assessment your new hobby. Trust us, it's more exciting than it sounds, especially when you see the results.

The Big Picture

Remember, sometimes the success of your business hinges on the potential and performance of your vendors. Choose wisely, and you're halfway to victory!

Takeaway:

Knowing your vendors well is like discovering a hidden strength you never knew you had.

<u>Positive Quote</u>

"Create Business Partners instead of Third-Party Vendors"

EXPERIENCE 48:
Know Your Bench – STRAIGHT, RELATE & ELATE

When we talk about ***"Know Your Bench,"*** your first thought might be about the employees currently in your organisation. But let's expand our horizons a bit. Today, your bench extends far beyond your office walls.

The Evolving Concept of 'Bench'

Think of your bench as a vast talent pool waiting to be tapped. It's not just about replacements or alternatives; it's about having the right resource at the right time from the right place.

Why Does Your Bench Matter?

Imagine having a pool of talent ready to step in when you need it most. That's what a well-known bench offers. It's about being prepared for any situation, whether it's unexpected vacancies, sudden project demands, or the need for specialised skills.

Building Your Dream Bench

So, how do you create this dream team of potential talent? Here are some strategies:

1. Stay Connected: Keep in touch with former employees and industry professionals. They're often your best resources.
2. Diversify Your Search: Don't limit yourself to one platform. Explore multiple channels to find hidden gems.
3. Embrace Flexibility: Consider freelancers, part-timers, and multi-skilled individuals. Flexibility is key in today's market.

The Power of a Strong Bench

Having a robust bench isn't just about filling positions. It's about confidence. Knowing you have access to quality talent can help you overcome unexpected challenges and manage work pressures effectively.

Action Steps:

1. Create an ex-employee network
2. Build relationships with resourceful professionals
3. Actively engage on various professional platforms
4. Keep your bench diverse and flexible

Remember: ***"Place Bench Well to accommodate quality numbers."***

Takeaway:

A well-known bench allows you to count on quality when it matters most. It's not just about numbers; it's about having the right people at your fingertips.

<u>Positive Quote</u>

"Create a Trusted Bench to Remain Trustworthy"

EXPERIENCE 49:
Know Your Techie – REMOVE, PROVE & IMPROVE

"Know Your Tech" has become more than just a catchphrase—it's a necessity. Let's find out why

The Tech Revolution

From start-ups to established corporations, technology is reshaping how we do business. Fintech, automation, digitalisation, robotics, machine learning, and AI are the building blocks of modern enterprises. But with great power comes great responsibility, and it's essential to understand both the potential and the pitfalls of these technologies.

Why Tech Matters

Imagine trying to navigate a new city without a map or GPS. That's what running a business without understanding technology feels like in today's world. Knowing your tech isn't just about staying current; it's about future-proofing your business.

The Human-Tech Balance

As we embrace technology, an important question arises: How do we balance human intelligence with technological capabilities? It's not about replacing humans but enhancing our abilities. Think of technology as a powerful tool in your toolkit, not a replacement for the craftsperson.

Considerations for Tech Adoption

When exploring new technologies, consider:

1. Need: Does this technology address a real need in your organisation?
2. Compatibility: How well does it integrate with your existing systems?
3. Cost vs. Benefit: What's the return on investment in terms of time and resources saved?
4. Security: How does it address potential cyber threats?

Remember, technology should solve problems, not create new ones.

Action Steps:

1. Assess your current technological landscape
2. Identify areas where technology can enhance efficiency
3. Evaluate the cost and time-saving potential of new tech
4. Invest in cybersecurity measures
5. Train your team to leverage new technologies effectively

Your Approach:

While embracing technology is crucial, it's important to approach it thoughtfully. As the saying goes, "Technology means Technical + Logical." It's not just about having the latest gadgets; it's about applying them logically to improve your business processes.

"Your Best Friend now is a Techie."

Takeaway:

As we rush to adopt new technologies, let's not forget that human creativity and insight are what drive technological innovation. The goal is to use technology to augment human capabilities, not replace them.

<u>Positive Quote</u>

"Reduce Redundancy by an increase in robust techies." – RRR

EXPERIENCE 50:
Be in the Law – Audit Trail – COMPLY, VERIFY & SIMPLIFY

As the journey progressed, we thought to add some spice to the experiential tour and introduce the concept of ***"Be in the Law."***

We all want to be in the Governance Frame by regularly watching and keeping an eye on changes/amendments in the various Acts related to our company in specific.

With the same analogy, compliance with change is the need of the hour to continue to be in the Frame of Law. To emphasise in this edition, the Audit Trail is mandatory feature for all accounting software for the Companies by MCA.

Audit Trail – basically a Log – record of events /transactions with a trail

Applicability – Immediate – with effect from 1st April 2023

Tick Box – Check the Accounting Software Feature & enable the feature of Audit Trail.

Non-Compliance – Sec 128 & Penalty –max 5 Lacs could be imposed.

Eligibility – ALL Companies registered under the Companies Act

Hope you found interesting to know some full forms for the short forms which we use quite often in our routine conversations, correspondence & so on.

"Have an eye on Law to avoid an eye by Law."

<u>Positive Quote</u>

"Know your boundaries to remain in boundaries."

Activity – Crossword Game

Across:

- Personal abilities or qualities that contribute to success (8 letters).

Down:

- Acronym for "Action, Reaction, Target" (3 letters).
- A common business tool for integrating new employees (4 letters).
- A goal or aim to achieve (6 letters).

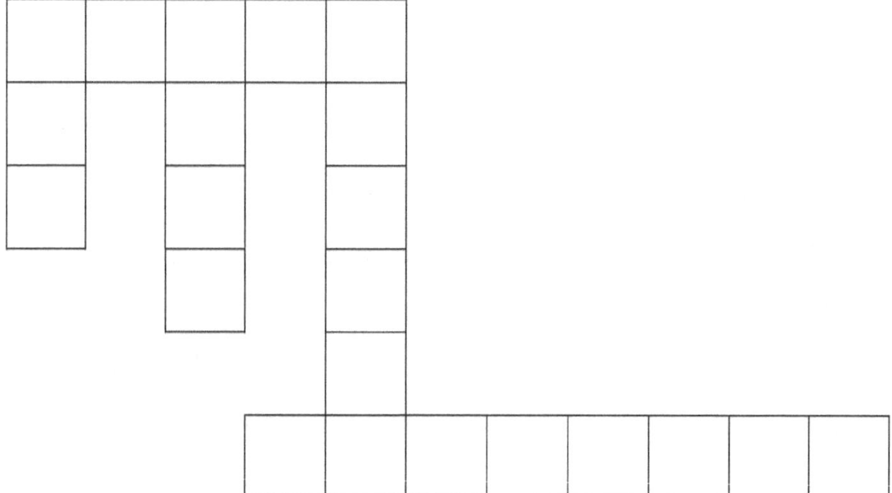

ABOUT THE AUTHOR

Shrenik Shah is a visionary entrepreneur having cutting edge eye on risk and evolved as an expert in Financial Crimes. Within span of 2 decades got nurtured and successfully appointed as an Independent director and strategic advisor for multiple companies. His sceptical approach had built a profound forensic practice. By developing innovative tools and techniques, Shrenik has not only set a new standard but has also pioneered advancements in the field of financial crime prevention.

A Fellow Member of the Institute of Chartered Accountants of India (ICAI) and a Certified Forensic Accountant and Fraud Investigator, Shrenik specializes in credit assessment, internal auditing, and forensic investigations.

Shrenik is the brainchild behind *MindMuneem,* a fraud detection and prevention measure for organizations that has successfully detected multiple fraud cases. He has also developed the *DigiFAR Tool* and *Vendor Scan* Theory designed to help organizations work with the right talent and minimize unnecessary losses. His innovative tools, including the Quinary Tripod Theory for credit assessment, showcase his commitment to improving business practices.

He has been an eminent speaker at multiple forums, including the National Forensic Sciences University (NFSU). This book distills his practical wisdom to help founders, aspiring entrepreneurs, and business enthusiasts navigate the modern business landscape. Readers will find not only valuable insights but also actionable strategies to apply in their own ventures.

Shrenik Shah is known as **SSS** – Sense, Solicit & Secure the Fraud

Note: The author or publisher does not endorse the tools mentioned.

For direct inquiries or to connect with Shrenik, please reach out via email at shrenik@sundayink.in

– CA Shrenik Shah
Founder & Partner at S N & Co.